Contents

I Can't Say That

Dear Auntie Beryl,
Thanks for the Christmas present.
It was lovely –
except twenty-four-piece puzzles are much
   too easy
for my age.
Mum's put it away for the baby.
I can't say that.

Dear Pen Pal,
Thanks for your letter.
You've got very nice handwriting.
Your holiday in the Bahamas sounded
   smashing.
We went to Weston this year
and it rained every single minute
except the afternoon we were going home.
I can't say that.

Dear Santa,
There's a whole string of presents
I'd really like to have
But why were the only ones I got last year
the little ones?
I can't say that.

Poetry

Edited by
Nick Whittaker
and Mick Connell

Published in association with
The Basic Skills Agency

Acknowledgements
Cover: David Hopkins
Illustrations: Mike Bell

The publishers would like to thank the following for their kind permission to
reproduce copyright material:

p1 'I Can't Say That' by Brian Morse from *Picnic on the Moon* © Brian Morse; p3
'Denis Law' by Gareth Owen © Gareth Owen 2000. Reproduced by permission of
the author c/o Rogers, Coleridge & White Ltd., 20 Powis Mews, London, W11
1JN; p5 'Don' Go Ova Dere' by Valerie Bloom © Valerie Bloom; p9 'Refugee
Mother and Child' by Chinua Achebe in *Beware Soul Brother* by kind permission of
Reed Educational and Professional Publishing; p11 'Woman Work' by Maya
Angelou in *And Still I Rise*, by kind permission of Virago Press; p13 'Just Jealous' by
Seni Seneviratne © Seni Seneviratne; p15 'Why' by Charles Causley by kind
permission of Macmillan; p17 'Harrybo' by Michael Rosen from *The Hypnotizer* by
kind permission of Scholastic Ltd; p20 'Fight' by Gareth Owen © Gareth Owen
2000. Reproduced by permission of the author c/o Rogers, Coleridge & White Ltd.;
p23 'Conversation Piece' by Gareth Owen © Gareth Owen 2000. Reproduced by
permission of the author c/o Rogers, Coleridge & White Ltd.; p26 'My Mother
Saw a Dancing Bear' by Charles Causley by kind permission of Macmillan; p28 'A
Flamingo' from *A Hippopotamusn't* by J. Patrick Lewis © 1990 by J. Patrick
Lewis. Used by permission of Dial Books for Young Readers, a division of
Penguin Putnum Inc. © J. Patrick; p29 'Studup' by Barrie Wade © Barrie Wade.

Every effort has been made to trace copyright holders of material reproduced in
this book. Any rights not acknowledged will be acknowledged in subsequent
printings if notice is given to the publisher.
Orders: please contact Bookpoint Ltd, 78 Milton Park, Abingdon, Oxon OX14
4TD. Telephone: (44) 01235 827720, Fax: (44) 01235 400454. Lines are open
from 9.00–6.00, Monday to Saturday, with a 24 hour message answering
service. Email address: orders@bookpoint.co.uk
British Library Cataloguing in Publication Data
A catalogue record for this title is available from The British Library

ISBN 0 340 78204 8

First published 2000
Impression number   10 9 8 7 6 5 4 3 2 1
Year   2005 2004 2003 2002 2001 2000

Typeset by Fakenham Photosetting Limited, Fakenham, Norfolk
Printed in Great Britain for Hodder & Stoughton Education, a division of
Hodder Headline Plc, 338 Euston Road, London NW1 3BH by Athenaeum
Press Ltd, Gateshead, Tyne and Wear.

Dear Teacher,
I think it's a very good idea
to practise writing letters,
but I already know
where to put the address and the date
and the postcode and the 'Yours sincerely',
and the 'With love from' –
it's the bit in between I find difficult.
I can't say that.

Brian Morse

Denis Law

I live at 14 Stanhope Street,
Me mum, me dad and me,
And three of us have made a gang,
John Stokes and Trev and me.

Our favourite day is Saturday;
We go Old Trafford way
And wear red colours in our coats
To watch United play.

We always stand behind the goal
In the middle of the roar.
The others come to see the game –
I come for Denis Law.

His red sleeves flap around his wrists,
He's built all thin and raw,
But the toughest backs don't stand a chance
When the ball's near Denis Law.

He's a whiplash when he's in control,
He can swivel like an eel,
And twist and sprint in such a way
It makes defences reel.

And when he's hurtling for the goal
I know he's got to score.
Defences may stop normal men –
They can't stop Denis Law.

We all race home when full time blows
To kick a tennis ball,
And Trafford Park is our back-yard,
And the stand is next door's wall.

Old Stokesey shouts, 'I'm Jimmy Greaves,'
And scores against the door,
And Trev shouts: 'I'll be Charlton,' –
But I am Denis Law.

Gareth Owen

Don' Go Ova Dere

Barry madda tell im
But Barry wouldn' hear,
Barry fada warn im
But Barry didn' care.
'Don' go ova dere, bwoy,
Don' go ova dere.'

Barry sista beg im
Barry pull her hair,
Barry brother bet im
'You can't go ova dere.'
'I can go ova dere, bwoy,
I can go ova dere.'

Barry get a big bag,
Barry climb de gate,
Barry granny call im
But Barry couldn' wait,
Im wan' get over dere, bwoy,
Before it get too late.

Barry see de plum tree
Im didn' see de bull,
Barry thinkin' bout de plums
'Gwine get dis big bag full.'
De bull get up an' shake, bwoy,
An gi de rope a pull.

De rope slip off de pole
But Barry didn' see,
De bull begin to stretch im foot dem
Barry climb de tree.
Barry start fe eat, bwoy,
Firs' one, den two, den three.

Barry nearly full de bag
An den im hear a soun'
Barry hol' de plum limb tight
An start fe look aroun'
When im see de bull, bwoy,
Im nearly tumble down.

cont.

Night a come, de bull naw move,
From unda dat plum tree,
Barry madda wondering
Whey Barry coulda be.
Barry getting tired, bwoy,
Of sittin' in dat tree.

An Barry dis realize
Him neva know before,
Sey de tree did full o' black ants
But now im know fe sure.
For some begin fe bite im, bwoy,
Den more, an more, an more.

De bull lay down fe wait it out,
Barry mek a jump,
De bag o' plum drop out de tree
An Barry hear a thump.
By early de nex' mawnin', bwoy,
Dat bull gwine have a lump.

De plum so frighten dat po' bull
Im start fe run too late,
Im a gallop afta Barry
But Barry jump de gate.
De bull jus' stamp im foot, bwoy,
Im yeye dem full o' hate.

When Barry ketch a im yard,
What a state im in!
Im los' im bag, im clothes mud up,
An mud deh pon im chin.
An whey de black ants bit im
Feba bull-frog skin.

Barry fada spank im,
Im mada sey im sin,
Barry sista scold im
But Barry only grin,
For Barry brother shake im head
An sey, 'Barry, yuh win!'

Valerie Bloom

Refugee Mother and Child

No Madonna and Child could touch
that picture of a mother's tenderness
for a son she soon would have to forget.

The air was heavy with odours
of diarrhoea of unwashed children
with washed-out ribs and dried-up
bottoms struggling in laboured
steps behind blown empty bellies. Most
mothers there had long ceased
to care but not this one; she held
a ghost smile between her teeth
and in her eyes the ghost of a mother's
pride as she combed the rust-coloured
hair left on his skull and then –
singing in her eyes – began carefully
to part it . . . In another life this

would have been a little daily
act of no consequence before his
breakfast and school; now she
did it like putting flowers
on a tiny grave.

Chinua Achebe

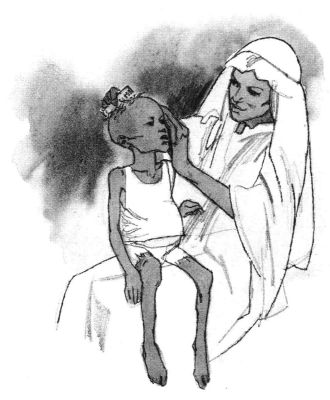

Woman Work

I've got the children to tend
The clothes to mend
The floor to mop
The food to shop
Then the chicken to fry
The baby to dry
I got company to feed
The garden to weed
I've got the shirts to press
The tots to dress
The cane to be cut
I gotta clean up this hut
Then see about the sick
And the cotton to pick.

Shine on me, sunshine
Rain on me, rain
Fall softly, dewdrops
And cool my brow again.

Storm, blow me from here
With your fiercest wind
Let me float across the sky
'Til I can rest again.

Fall gently, snowflakes
Cover me with white
Cold icy kisses and
Let me rest tonight.

Sun, rain, curving sky
Mountain, oceans, leaf and stone
Star shine, moon glow
You're all that I can call my own.

Maya Angelou

Just Jealous

'They're just jealous'
My mum used to say to me
When I came crying
Home from school
Saying they'd called me 'nigger'
And it made sense then
Because I liked my brown skin.

But it didn't make sense
In later years
When a man drove his car
At me on a beach
Shouting 'black bastard'
He wasn't 'just jealous'
He was angry that I'd answered back.

Yet I can't say
She was wrong to say it
Thinking today of a black child in care
Scrubbing her skin till it bleeds
Trying to make it white
I wanted to say
'Didn't anyone ever tell you
That your black skin is nice
And they're all just jealous.'

And when my own daughter
comes home from school
Asking why they call her 'Paki'
Shall I say 'just jealous'
Or try to explain
The centuries of racism
That are heaped behind that word?

And will it make more sense
Than what my mum said to me?

Seni Seneviratne

Why?

Why do you turn your head, Susanna,
And why do you swim your eye?
It's only the children on Bellman Street
Calling, *A penny for the guy!*

Why do you look away, Susanna,
As the children wheel him by?
It's only a dummy in an old top-hat
And a fancy jacket and tie.

Why do you take my hand, Susanna,
As the pointing flames jump high?
It's only a bundle of sacking and straw.
Nobody's going to die.

Why is your cheek so pale, Susanna,
As the whizzbangs flash and fly?
It's nothing but a rummage of paper and rag
Strapped to a stick you spy.

Why do you say you hear, Susanna,
The sound of a last, long sigh?
And why do you say it won't leave your head
No matter how hard you try?

Best let me take you home, Susanna.
Best on your bed to lie.
It's only a dummy in an old top-hat.
Nobody's going to die.

Charles Causley

Harrybo

Once my friend Harrybo
Came to school crying.
We said:
What's the matter?
What's the matter?
And he said
His grandad had died.

So we didn't know what to say.

Then I said:
How did he die?
And he said:
He was standing on St Pancras station
Waiting for the train
And he just fell over and died.

Then he started crying again.

He was a nice man
Harrybo's grandad.
He had a shed with tins full of screws in it.

Mind you,
My gran was nice too
She gave me and my brother
A red shoe horn each.
Maybe Harrybo's grandad gave
Harrybo a red shoe horn.

Dave said:
My hamster died as well
So everyone said:
Shhhh.

And Dave said:
I was only saying.
And I said:
My gran gave me a red shoe horn.

cont.

Rodge said:
I got a pair of trainers for Christmas.
And Harrybo said:
You can get ones without laces.
And we all said:
Yeah, that's right, Harrybo, you can.

Any other day,
We'dve said:
Of course you can, we know that, you fool.
But that day
We said:
Yeah, that's right, Harrybo, yeah, you can.

Michael Rosen

Fight

'A scrap! A scrap!'
The tingle in the scalp
starts us running.

The shout drains
our playground just as though
a plug was pulled

here in the space
in which two twisted, furious
bodies writhe.

Rules will not prise
these savages apart.
No ref will interpose

with shouts of 'Break!'
This contest has one single,
vicious round

of grab and grapple,
wrestle, thump and scrabble,
flail and scratch.

cont.

We take no sides.
Our yells are wolves howling
for blood of any kind.

Our fingers clench.
The thrill claws in our throats
like raging thirst.

The whistle shrills
and splits our pack. The circle
heaves and shatters.

The fighters still
are blind and deaf, won't hear
or see until,

parted, they go limp
as cubs drawn by the scruff
from some hot lair.

Now they are tame.
Standing outside Sir's room
grinning their shame.

Chastened, we feel
the snarls of wildness
stifle in us.

Gareth Owen

Conversation Piece

Late again Blenkinsop?
What's the excuse this time?
Not my fault sir.
Who's fault is it then?
Grandma's sir.
Grandma's. What did she do?
She died sir.
Died?
She's seriously dead all right sir.
That makes four grandmothers this term.
And all on P.E. days Blenkinsop.
I know. It's very upsetting sir.
How many grandmothers have you got
    Blenkinsop?
Grandmothers sir? None sir.
None?
All dead sir.

And what about yesterday Blenkinsop?

What about yesterday sir?

You missed maths.

That was the dentist sir.

The dentist died?

No sir. My teeth sir.

You missed the test Blenkinsop.

I'd been looking forward to it too sir.

Right, line up for P.E.

Can't sir.

No such word as can't. Why can't you?

No kit sir.

Where is it?

Home sir.

What's it doing at home?

Not ironed sir.

cont.

Couldn't you iron it?
Can't do it sir.
Why not?
My hand sir.
Who usually does it?
Grandma sir.
Why couldn't she do it?
Dead sir.

Gareth Owen

My Mother Saw a Dancing Bear

My mother saw a dancing bear
By the schoolyard, a day in June.
The keeper stood with chain and bar
And whistle-pipe, and played a tune.

And bruin lifted up its head
And lifted up its dusty feet,
And all the children laughed to see
It caper in the summer heat.

They watched as for the Queen it died.
They watched it march. They watched it halt.
They heard the keeper as he cried,
'Now, roly-poly!' 'Somersault!'

And then, my mother said, there came
The keeper with a begging-cup,
The bear with burning coat of fur,
Shaming the laughter to a stop.

cont.

They paid a penny for the dance,
But what they saw was not the show;
Only, in bruin's aching eyes,
Far-distant forests, and the snow.

Charles Causley

A Flamingo

```
                    F l a m i n g
                                   o
          A
            i
              s

                  a

                  l
                  o
                  n
                  g
              o o o o o o
        o o o            o o
      o                      o
    c                          o
                                 l
      d   r   i   n   k
              o
              f
                p
              s
              o
              m     i
              e
              t         n
              h
              i
              n       k
              g
```

J. Patrick Lewis

Studup

'Owayer?'
'Imokay.'
'Gladtwearit.'
'Howbowchew?'
'Reelygrate.'
'Binwaytinlong?'
'Longinuff.'
'Owlongubineer?'
'Boutanour.'
'Thinkeelturnup?'
'Aventaclue.'
'Dewfancyim?'
'Sortalykim.'
'Wantadrinkorsummat?'
'Thanksilestayabit.'
'Soocherself.'
'Seeyalater.'
'Byfernow.'

Barrie Wade